The History of the Personal Computer

The History of the Personal Computer

Josepha Sherman

$\mathcal{W}\!atts$ LIBRARY™

Franklin Watts
A Division of Scholastic Inc.
New York • Toronto • London • Auckland • Sydney
Mexico City • New Delhi • Hong Kong
Danbury, Connecticut

Note to readers: Definitions for words in **bold** can be found in the Glossary at the back of this book.

Photographs © 2003: Computer History Museum: 16; Corbis Images: 23, 27 (Bettmann), 49 (Firefly Productions), 6 (Kevin R. Morris), 14 (National Photo Company), 42 (Jose Luis Pelaez), 48 (Reuters New Media), 32 (Doug Wilson), 8 (Ed Young); Folio, Inc./ Everett C. Johnson: 33; H. Armstrong Roberts, Inc.: 24; Hulton|Archive/Getty Images: 19; Intel Museum: 34; North Wind Picture Archives: 9; Photo Researchers, Inc./Novastock: 2; PhotoEdit/Mark Richards: 39; Photri Inc.: 45 (Mark E. Gibson), 28, 29, 30; Smithsonian Institution, Washington, DC: cover; Stock Boston/ Peter Southwick: 46; Stock Montage, Inc.: 10, 11, 12; Superstock, Inc.: 20, 21; Woodfin Camp & Associates/ Bernard Gotfryd: 22.

The photograph on the cover shows the Altair 8800, the first personal computer. The photograph opposite the title page shows one of the early models of personal computers.

Library of Congress Cataloging-in-Publication Data

Sherman, Josepha.
    The history of the personal computer / by Josepha Sherman
        p. cm. — (Watts library)
    Includes bibliographical references and index.
    Summary: Discusses the inventors and scientists who contributed to the development of computers, and more recently, personal computers.
    ISBN 0-531-12166-6 (lib. bdg.)   0-531-16213-3 (pbk.)
    1. Microcomputers—History—Juvenile literature. [1. Microcomputers—History. 2. Computers—History.] I. Title. II. Series.
QA76.23.S52 2003
004.16—dc21   2002008507

Contents

The abacus is still used for calculating in parts of Asia and the Middle East, and some parts of Russia.

Chapter One

Before the Computer

Some people believe that we might never have had computers if it hadn't been for the need to count things. The earliest method of counting was probably the simplest, keeping track of items on fingers and toes. Then followed more complicated methods, such as **tallying** up things using pebbles as counters, and later writing numbers down.

As the centuries passed, the need to perform more and more complicated computations grew. Figures added up on

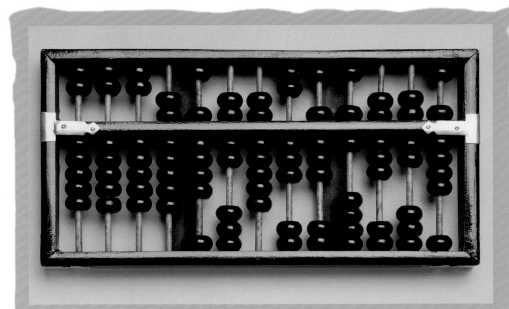

What Is an Abacus?

The basic abacus is simply a frame of wood or metal strung with wires. Each wire has beads on it. All the beads on a wire have the same value, based on the decimal system of tens. For instance, each bead on one wire might represent the number 1, while all those on another wire might represent the number 10. Numbers are added together on the abacus by grouping beads together, and subtraction is done by separating groups of beads. By moving beads in more complicated patterns, it is possible to do multiplication and division as well.

paper by even the fastest math wizard just weren't calculated quickly enough or with sufficient accuracy. In China, possibly as far back as five thousand years ago, some brilliant person—we don't know who—invented the abacus. Forms of it were also used in Greece and Rome. This hand-operated device was the first mechanical aid to computing and the first known step toward the development of the modern computer.

The Dawn of Computers

In 1642, Blaise Pascal watched his tax-collector father struggling with figures in France. Being a clever young man and feeling sorry for his father, the eighteen-year-old Pascal promptly invented a device to help him. Called the Pascaline, it was an early form of adding machine. About the size of a shoebox, it had eight windows on its top. Behind each window was a small drum with two rows of numbers on it, one black row for addition and one red row for subtraction. Below

Along with the Pascaline, Pascal also invented the syringe and the hydraulic press.

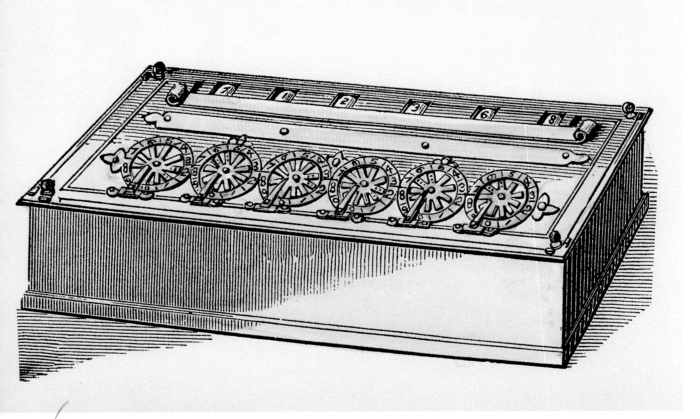

9

The Jacquard Loom

In 1801 inventor Joseph-Marie Jacquard wanted to make weaving more efficient. As a solution, he invented the Jacquard loom. Thick cards punched with rectangular holes controlled the patterns being woven. This loom wasn't a computer, but Jacquard's idea of storing information on punched cards was later used in early computers.

This photograph shows Babbage's Analytical Engine.

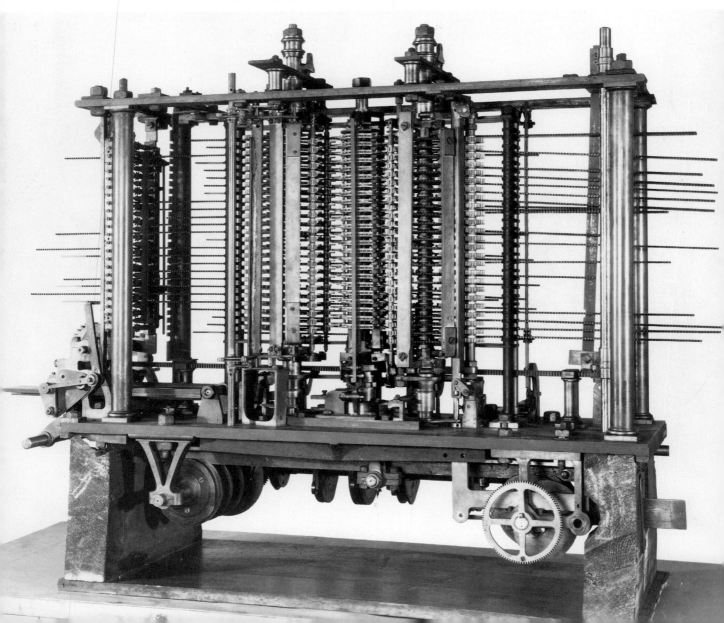

each window was a small cogged wheel. To add or subtract, you turned each little wheel, which in turn rotated the drums to reveal or cover numbers in the windows.

The start of what we know as computers began in the mid-1800s with Charles Babbage. Born on December 26, 1791, in London, England, he grew up at the dawn of the Industrial Revolution, when everyone was hunting for more efficient, more mechanized ways to work. Babbage became a scientist-inventor, and he is called the Father of Computing for a very good reason. He designed the first plans for a true computer. He called his devices "Calculating Engines." The original design in 1820 or 1821 was for the Difference Engine. In 1832 he came up with a more complicated version called the Analytical Engine, which used punch cards and included many of the features that appear in modern computers.

Babbage's assistant was Augusta Ada Byron, countess of Lovelace and daughter of the English poet Lord Byron. Byron was the perfect aide for Babbage, since she understood the machines' principles as well as he did, and designed the instruction routines that would be fed into

Augusta Ada Byron, who first met Babbage in 1833, went on to become a competent mathematician. This was considered most unusual for a woman in that era, since none of the sciences were considered suitable occupations for a woman.

The Father of Computing

While his engines were never made in his lifetime, Charles Babbage had a great many other achievements in his busy life. Babbage pioneered lighthouse signaling and developed a system of mathematical code breaking. In addition, he was an important political economist and a leading figure in London society.

them. This makes the countess the first female computer programmer. In the 1980s, the U.S. Department of Defense named a programming language "Ada" in her honor.

Unfortunately, Babbage designed these early computing engines in the early 1800s. Later tests in London and elsewhere have proven that the machines would have worked. However, during Babbage's time, the technology available to build the devices was primitive, and each part had to be handcrafted. Babbage died in 1871, without ever seeing any of his Calculating Engines in operation.

People worked as census takers and went door-to-door collecting information.

Chapter Two

The First Computers

Toward the end of the 1800s, the United States grew rapidly. New births and new immigrants caused the population to increase, and it became difficult to take a **census** to discover just who and where everybody was. The census of 1880 took a tedious seven years to complete, and of course was out of date by the time it was finally finished. The United States didn't want the next census to take even longer.

Inventor Herman Hollerith set to work on a faster way of tallying information.

Hollerith's machine helped speed up the process of calculating census data.

Hollerith and IBM

Besides his contributions to the creation of the computer, there was also another connection linking Hollerith to the coming computer age. Hollerith's Tabulating Machine Company, which he founded in 1896, became part of the International Business Machines (IBM) Corporation in 1924. Later IBM would become a major force in the development of the computer.

He came up with a method that encoded data onto special cards through a series of punched holes. The machine he invented then read the cards as they were passed through electrical contacts. Not only was this system helpful in figuring out statistics, it laid some of the groundwork for the development of the digital computer.

Hollerith's machine was used in the 1890 census—and thanks to it, the raw census count was finished in only six weeks. It took another two and a half years to finalize the results.

In the first four decades of the 1900s, there wasn't much advancement in computer science. The main problem wasn't a lack of intelligence or inspiration. It was the same problem that Charles Babbage encountered with his Calculating Engines. The technology of the time wasn't powerful enough. Machines relied on **vacuum tubes** to control the flow of electricity.

Vacuum tubes worked perfectly well for early radios. They also were used in the first televisions, which appeared at the end of the 1930s. These early devices had to be quite large to

A Useful Vacuum

The vacuum tube owes its discovery to Thomas Alva Edison and the first lightbulb, which consisted of a wire **filament** inside a glass from which all the air had been drawn, leaving a vacuum. When electricity passed through the filament, the wire heated up and glowed, but the vacuum kept it from burning up. The English physicist John Ambrose Fleming discovered that the process could also be used to detect radio waves and to convert them to electricity. He developed a two-element vacuum tube known as a diode. In 1906 the American inventor Lee De Forest added a third **electrode** into the vacuum tube. He had invented the triode vacuum tube, which could be used as both an **amplifier** and a switch.

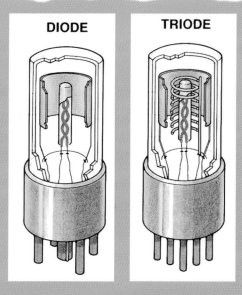

accommodate the bulky vacuum tubes. The tubes had to be handled with care because they were fragile. They also tended to overheat, and they burned out frequently.

Computers and Warfare

When World War II began, many advances were made in technology. The Germans and the Allies were in a race to be the first to develop computers to help in planning war strategy. In 1941, Konrad Zuse, a German engineer, invented the Z3, a programmable **calculator**, to help design airplanes and missiles. In 1943 the British invented a top-secret computer, Colossus, to decode enemy messages. No one outside of

British military intelligence even knew Colossus existed until well after the war had ended.

Meanwhile, the United States was making its own discoveries. In 1944 engineer Howard H. Aiken, working with IBM, invented a computer-calculator, the Mark I. It was slow by today's standards, taking up to five seconds to solve a calculation, but it worked. Meanwhile, John Presper Eckert and John W. Mauchly were designing a faster computer. They were part of a collaboration between the United States government and the University of Pennsylvania. Their 1945 creation was called

John Mauchly (left) and John Eckert stand by their computer creation, ENIAC. Eckert points to some of the thousands of vacuum tubes that the ENIAC required.

ENIAC, the Electronic Numerical Integrator And Computer, and it was a monster. ENIAC was a thousand times faster than the Mark I, but it used 18,000 vacuum tubes, took up 1,800 square feet (167 square meters), weighed 30 tons, and used enough power to dim lights in a whole section of Philadelphia. It was programmed by plugging in electric cords and setting thousands of switches. Not exactly the most practical of computers, but it paved the way for the next generation.

In 1945, the ENIAC team working with John von Neumann, at the University of Pennsylvania, designed the Electronic Discrete Variable Automatic Computer (EDVAC). Finished in 1952, this new monster computer was unique in that it was the first with a memory to hold a stored program as well as the data typed into it. This meant that unlike ENIAC this computer did not have to be re-wired to run the next program.

Eckert and Mauchly left the University of Pennsylvannia in 1946 and founded the Electronic Control Company (ECC), the first computer company. ECC, which was later renamed the Eckert-Mauchly Computer

Computers in the Movies

Anyone curious about what early, gigantic computers really looked like in action should watch almost any science fiction movie from the late 1950s and early 1960s. Those long white walls with the huge rotating tapes and blinking lights give a pretty good idea of what was considered high-tech for computing in that era.

This photograph shows an UNIVAC computer. It was designed to perform statistical calculations.

Typewriter Company Buys UNIVAC

In 1950, Eckert and Mauchly's company was bought by Remington Rand, a company famous for manufacturing typewriters. Remington Rand sold the UNIVAC to organizations, such as General Electric and the United States Census Bureau.

Company, designed the Universal Automatic Computer (UNIVAC). Like the computers before it, UNIVAC was the size of a very large room, thanks to the large vacuum tubes it needed. It used magnetic drums the size of car tires for storage. It weighed some 16,000 pounds (7,257 kilograms), used 5,000 vacuum tubes, and could perform about 1,000 calculations per second. What made the UNIVAC different was that it was the first American commercially available computer.

The UNIVAC was too big and expensive to be bought by most companies. This generation of computers was not going to be the answer to everyone's technology needs. However, many people were working to improve computer technology. In 1945, Bell Telephone Laboratories set up a research team to find an alternative to vacuum tubes to serve as electronic switches in the system's circuits. In 1947 the team, led by William Shockley and including Walter Brattain and John Bardeen, announced a breakthrough. Almost by accident, they had created an **amplifying circuit**, a device that strengthens an electrical current, that seemed to work. Instead of needing a vacuum tube, this small **transistor**, known as a semiconductor, which looked like today's transistor battery, used the

$$V = \frac{4\pi\rho}{\varepsilon} \, \ell^2$$

$$\rho = 10^{14} \times 4.8 \times 1$$

$$= 4.8 \times 10^4$$

Shockley, Brattain, and Bardeen worked together to find a replacement for the bulky vacuum tube.

Research Rewarded

The work of William Shockley, Walter Brattain, and John Bardeen on the development of the semiconductor was considered such a significant achievement that it earned them an award from the Nobel Prize committee. The three men were given the Nobel Prize in Physics in 1956.

element **germanium** to transmit electric current. They had found something small, cheap, and powerful called a solid object. This object led to the term **"solid-state technology,"** a technology with none of the problems of the vacuum tube.

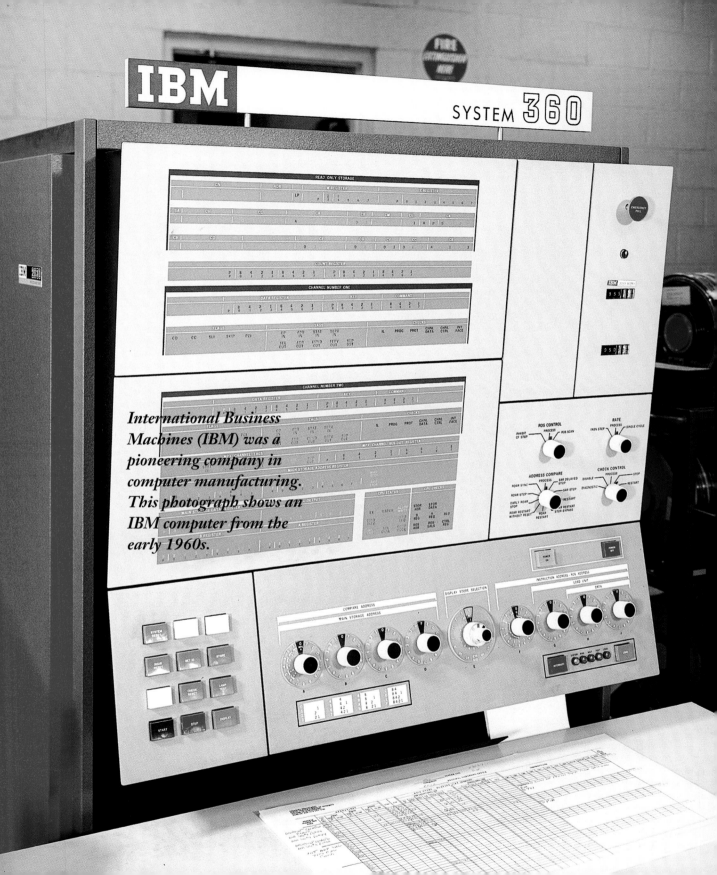

International Business Machines (IBM) was a pioneering company in computer manufacturing. This photograph shows an IBM computer from the early 1960s.

Chapter Three

The Computer Evolves

Computers were gaining a foothold in the United States in the 1950s. In 1953 IBM was the first to design a mass-produced computer, the IBM 650. By December 1954, five hundred IBM 650s had been made. This may not seem like very many, but it marked the first time a computer could be easily produced. IBM also designed the first solid-state computer—one using transistors rather than vacuum tubes—in 1959. This was the IBM 7090. With each new design, the machines became smaller and, at the same time, more powerful. They were still large, though. The IBM 650, for instance, had a **central processing unit** (CPU) that was 5 feet (1.5 meters) by 3 feet (0.9 m) by 6 feet (1.8 m), and weighed 1,966 pounds (891.7 kg). Eventually all large, general purpose computers that could be shared by many users came to be known as **mainframe computers**. The word "mainframe" is thought to have come from the metal frames that the computer electronic components were mounted on.

Some of these machines were intended for big business. The main user of computers in the 1950s, though, was still the government. This was the era of the Cold War, after all, the fierce rivalry between the United States and what was then the Soviet Union headed by Russia.

The Cold War fueled the development of the first supercomputers, computers that could perform calculations far more swiftly than any earlier machines. These were designed by IBM and a rival company, Sperry-Rand, and were intended for use by the Atomic Energy Commission and for atomic energy laboratories. IBM's computer was called Stretch, and

Uneasy Times

The Cold War, which lasted from 1945 to the 1990s, never heated up into actual combat, fortunately. However, everyone was worried that it might. Since the discovery of atomic power and the atom bomb, a dangerous arms race had been going on. Each side wanted to have more, and more powerful, weapons than the other.

Sperry-Rand designed the LARC, which stood for Livermore Atomic Research Computer.

Those computers were too expensive to be used by businesses or universities. In fact, only two LARCs were ever put into use. Businesses and universities alike started demanding less expensive computers for research and record keeping. They wanted smaller, more versatile computers that could be used for more than one purpose. Through the 1960s, several companies, including IBM and Sperry-Rand, as well as Honeywell and others, started designing computers to meet the growing demand.

After creating these new computers, a new problem arose. Now that so many companies and universities owned computers, they wanted to be able to share files between their computers. In 1964, IBM made a breakthrough. Its System/360 series of computers were compatible with each other. This meant that files could be shared between them. It seems like a pretty obvious feature today, but in 1964, this was a real breakthrough that saved hours of work.

Businesses were happy, and so were universities. By 1965, many of them owned computers that could process financial data and keep records for them. The public knew something about computers by now, too, at least from what they read in newspapers and saw on television. The public perceived computers as big, almost magical machines that could do nearly anything.

This generation of computers was still made up of larger

Chess Players

In 1957 the first full game of chess was written for an IBM 704. By 1966 university students were setting up chess matches of computer versus computer, and a Russian chess program defeated a Stanford IBM 7090 program. In 1967 a computer named Mac Hack VI became the first chess-playing machine to beat a human opponent. The computer was made an honorary member of the United States Chess Federation.

machines than few people could use with the exception of large business or university personnel. Use time was limited for students. There was still a need for computers for the small business—and for the individual businessperson, scholar, or scientist.

There were some technical problems to be solved. While the transistor was a great improvement over the vacuum tube, it still gave off enough heat to damage computer parts, causing failures of every type—from not running files to not running at all. Scientists already knew that the composition of quartz rock cooled things down by allowing heat to safely **dissipate**. So computer scientists began working on ways to include quartz in computer circuits. In 1958, engineer Jack Kirby, working for Texas Instruments, designed the integrated circuit (IC), which integrated three electronic components onto one small silicon disc made from quartz. In 1959, Texas Instruments and Fairchild Semiconductor formally announced the development of the integrated circuit. The heat problem was solved, and the integrated circuit also helped reduce the size of computers and enhanced their speed.

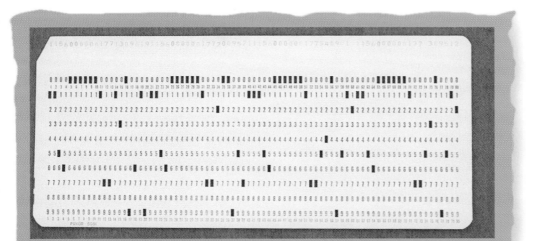

Carded

In the 1960s there were no such things as **floppy disks** or **Compact Discs** (CDs). Students who wanted to access a school computer used punch cards, computer cards with holes punched in certain positions to represent data, or information. There was always a danger of these cards, which were made of cardboard, being damaged.

Floppy Disks

Why is a computer's storage device called a floppy disk? Some of the original 8-inch (20.3-centimeter) disks weren't in any sort of protective cover. They really were floppy! Such disks could easily be damaged by being bent. The 5.25-inch (13.3-cm) disks introduced in 1976 were floppy, too. But the most recent design, the 3.5-inch (8.9-cm) disk, comes in a protective plastic casing. These disks are far from floppy, and are less easily damaged.

From the 1960s into the 1970s, several companies realized that there was a genuine market for smaller computers. Mainframes were just too big for most offices, and there were more and more small businesses and individuals who wanted their own small computers. Scientists began working to fit more and more circuits onto each disc, or **computer chip**. Storage devices were also becoming smaller and more efficient, too. The original floppy disks, dating from the early 1970s, were read-only. This meant that the information on them, which was usually code for a mainframe computer, couldn't be altered. A technician wanting to update the code would simply replace the disk. The storage capacity of one of these read-only disks was less than 100 **kilobytes**. By 1973, that had changed to 250 kilobytes. The drive now had read/write capability, too, which meant that changes could be made directly to the disk.

The Birth of the PC

In January 1975, the magazine *Popular Electronics* announced the birth of the first true personal computer, or PC, one that was meant for an individual user. The magazine featured an article about the MITS Altair 8800 microcomputer, which could be built from a kit.

Nobody really expected the wild reaction that this article received. The article caused great excitement among readers, many of whom were inspired to get involved with the new computers. In fact, that article marked the beginning of a whole new computer industry.

Soon companies sprang up to design rival computers. There was Radio Shack's TRS-80 in 1977, which quickly became a highly popular home computer—though it didn't have a disk drive and needed a cassette recorder for program storage. There were the Atari computers—which were great

Birth of a Giant

The news about the Altair micro-computer also changed the lives of two young men, Bill Gates and Paul Allen. In the 1970s they both became fascinated with computers while in school. They realized that all those new personal computers were going to need **software** to run them. So Gates and Allen quit college to start the computer software business that became the software giant Microsoft.

for games but weren't too useful for anything else, since they didn't have enough power for complicated work.

Founded by Steve Jobs and Steve Wozniak, Apple Computer released its first computer, the Apple II, in 1977. It has been called the first true personal computer, since it was factory built, inexpensive, and easy to learn and to use. It used a completely different operating system than other personal computers.

More successful than the other PCs was the Commodore

64, introduced in 1982, which quickly became the best-selling PC. The Commodore 64 succeeded because it had features that the other computers did not. It had a relatively large memory (though unbelievably small by today's standards), as well as good graphics and inexpensive floppy disks.

Commodore 64 was one of the most popular early personal computers.

Bytes

The "64" in the Commodore 64's name stood for 64 kilobytes, or 64K, of memory. A kilobyte is a little over a thousand **bytes**. A byte is the basic unit for representing data in the computer and consists of eight bits. By comparison, most of today's PCs have many gigabytes of memory. A gigabyte is more than one billion bytes more than the Commodore 64 could ever boast.

The 4004 chip kicked off the drive to create smaller and faster computer chips.

Chapter Four

PCs Catch On

Computers might have remained bulky mainframes if it hadn't been for a company called Intel, which designs computer chips. In 1971, Intel designed the 4004 chip. This chip made the pocket calculator possible, allowing everyone to carry around the calculating power of a computer. A handheld calculator isn't a full computer, but the success of the 4004 chip gave Intel the inspiration and funding to work on better, smaller, and faster computer chips. Still, there was no real progress in the design of PCs for almost ten years.

A Very Good Year for Computing

Then the breakthrough happened. In 1981, after several months of top-secret work under the code name "Acorn," IBM launched its first PC, running on an Intel 8088 **microprocessor** and using Microsoft software. Even though microprocessors had been available since 1971, this was the first time anyone had been able to successfully design a practical PC. The speed of 8088 seems amazingly slow today, when computers zip along, processing data at higher and higher speeds every year—but it was amazingly fast in 1981.

Another breakthrough in 1981 was the invention of the Osborne 1 by Adam Osborne, a computer engineer and writer. The Osborne 1 was the first portable computer and included all the hardware of a regular PC. It was cheap, too, selling for $1,795. Unfortunately, it was heavy, weighing a hefty 30 pounds (13.6 kg). The Osborne Company went bankrupt after only a few years, but other computer companies were inspired to start designing smaller and more portable computers.

Yet another breakthrough in 1981 was the appearance of the first nonbusiness modem, designed by Hayes Micromodem

Computer Speeds

How fast is fast? In 1993, Intel introduced its Pentium chip. One chip, smaller than the first joint of a forefinger, held almost three and a half million transistors, nearly three times the number contained in its predecessor, the 80486 chip. The 486 was well over three times faster than the original 8088 chip. New versions of the Pentium II, III, and IV are much faster than the original Pentium.

for the PC. It was only 300 **baud**, which is almost a crawl com-
pared to today's modems and high-speed Digital Subscriber
Lines (DSL), but it provided the first opportunity for new PC
owners to go online. And the first online service, Compuserve,
was ready for them.

Adam Osborne shows off his creation, the Osborne 1—the first portable personal computer.

The Race Is On

The IBM personal computers were expensive. Other companies set out to create computers based on the IBM design. Because IBM had never wanted to patent the concept of the PC—that is, legally reserve the design so no one could copy it—personal computers that were similar to IBM PCs, called PC clones, started appearing on the market. In the 1980s there were no fewer than a hundred different companies racing to have their PCs ready for sale. The first to have a PC clone on the market was Compaq, in 1982, closely followed by Radio Shack. Many of the hastily put-together companies didn't survive for more than a year or two at the most.

Many of the early manufacturers of PCs are no longer around, but some of the most successful early computer companies are still in existence. These include Compaq and Radio Shack. The two biggest computer makers, Dell Computers and Gateway Computers, got their start in the mid-

1980s. Dell was founded by Michael Dell in 1984, and Gateway Computers was founded by Ted Waitt and Mike Hammond in 1985.

While the market was crowded with computer manufacturers, one computer chipmaker, Intel, dominated the computer-chip market. There were other computer chipmakers, such as Motorola, Cyrix, and AMD, but Intel quickly captured the largest share of the market, making computer chips for all brands of PCs. To date, Intel still remains the world's largest manufacturer of computer chips.

Technicians examine a computer chip.

Microsoft was also thriving during the 1980s. The company created Microsoft DOS (Disk Operating System). Microsoft DOS was launched officially on August 12, 1981, and quickly spread in popularity. It became the major operating system for PCs through the 1980s.

While the Microsoft DOS (MS-DOS) operating system had no competitors in the PC world, the PC itself did have one. Apple Computer's new line of personal computers, the Macintosh, first appeared in 1984. The Mac, as it quickly became known, didn't use MS-DOS. It had its own operating system and its own way of doing things. It made use of a computer mouse, which DOS didn't, and included "icons," small images on the computer screen that represented the programs on the computer. If the Mac user clicked with his or her mouse on an icon, the program would open. Mac users loved it. PC users looked down on the icons as being childish.

Love them or hate them, though, there was no denying that those icons were convenient. With DOS, you had to remember long strings of letters and symbols, and type them in. With those icons, you just pointed a cursor and clicked a mouse button. In November 1985, Microsoft launched its first version of Windows, an operating system that also used convenient icons.

Steve Jobs shows off an early version of the Macintosh computer.

In the early 1980s, more and more people decided to buy personal computers.

Chapter Five

The Future of Computing

In 1981, 2 million PCs were sold. In 1982 that number had jumped to 5.5 million. *Time* Magazine named the PC its 1983 "Man of the Year." But at first many people were afraid of computers. After all, this was a new and expensive technology. What if they pressed the wrong button and deleted everything? What if they broke the machine?

Along with fear, some people experienced computer frustration. Computers and versions of software changed constantly during the 1980s and 1990s. People couldn't keep up with all the upgrades. By the end of the 1990s many people didn't want to bother. The joke about computers was that they were "obsolete the second they left the factory." Besides, people had come to realize that a good computer could last three to five years. There was no reason to rush out and spend money on a new one when the old one still worked perfectly.

There's been a slowdown in the computer industry as a result. Fewer new computers are being sold, and fewer upgrades of software are successful. No one knows if the slowdown will continue, or if people will ever go back to buying every new version of software or latest technology that the computer sellers offer.

Changing Our Lives

This slowdown doesn't mean that personal computers are going away. Personal computers have changed the way we work, partly because computers have shrunk. Companies like IBM and Sony, to name only two, have come up with tiny computers called notebooks—since they're no bigger than a real notebook—and have true Pentium power yet weigh under

Notebook computers have made it easier for people to use their computers almost anywhere.

Through their personal computers, people use the Internet to reach all across the world.

3 pounds (1.4 kg). As a result, people can take their work or play with them when they travel. It's not unusual to see several men and women typing away on their notebook computers on airplanes or trains. It's also not unusual to find docking ports for these computers in hotels. These ports are places in hotel rooms where someone can plug in a computer and even access the Internet. There are also access ports that allow people on airplanes to use their computers to go online.

Even astronauts use PCs. They have portable computers aboard every Space Shuttle flight and aboard the International Space Station, Space Station Alpha, as well. These are slightly larger computers than the notebooks, called laptops because a laptop computer often rests on a user's lap. The astronauts can even send and receive e-mail.

The personal computer has made it possible for us to hook up to the entire world on the Internet. All it takes is a computer, a modem, a phone line, and a service provider, and you can talk to friends around the world, buy stuff without leaving your home, or even watch live shots from space in real time. People no longer have to work at nine-to-five jobs in an office. With a PC, modem, and fax machine, someone can stay in touch with the home office yet be in a hotel or even on a beach. This is called telecommuting, and for many people it's becoming a very convenient way to work.

You don't need a full PC to access the Internet. Personal digital assistants and cellular phones can link you to the Internet. Some of the newest versions of these devices allow you to send and receive e-mail as well.

Future Dreams

What will the world of computing be like in the future? We already have partly computerized houses, such as the one that Microsoft's Bill Gates has had built for himself and his family. Lights can be programmed to go on or off by themselves. Houses can be programmed to "recognize" someone at the

Computer technology is a key part of Bill Gates's home.

door. There are plans for computerized refrigerators that will know when we're low on milk—and houses that will even do the ordering of supplies for us. No one is sure yet how totally computerized a house should be. It remains to be seen whether people will want their homes to have any control over their lives.

Will we be wearing computerized clothing? Some jackets, shirts, and glasses that are also computer devices have already been designed, but they aren't very attractive. In the near future some designer may yet figure out a way to work computers and other devices directly into ordinary clothing, so that they can't be seen. Computerized clothing might have a medical use. For example, a "smart shirt" could keep track of

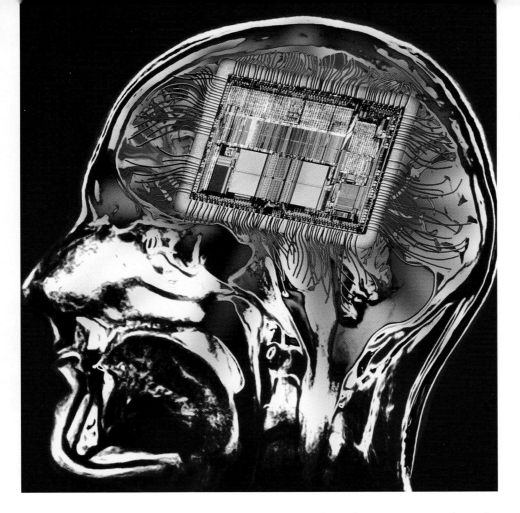

Could computers become a part of you someday?

someone's heart rate, or be able to notify a doctor immediately in an emergency. There might also be entertainment uses for computerized clothing, such as jackets that let you hear music or glasses that instantaneously show you stock reports or restaurant guides. There's a big question about such clothing. Will the public actually want it?

Another question is whether we will someday all have implanted sockets in our heads. This would allow us to join with our computers and input data directly into our brains. That seems the stuff of science fiction, and it may not be possible, or healthy, for that matter. In the real world, some steps have already been taken in this direction. There have been experiments with computer chip implants that stimulate nerves and help people with artificial limbs move more naturally.

Since no one predicted the coming of the PC, no one can accurately tell what future forms of computing will be like. One thing seems certain. Whatever shape the future takes, some form of PCs will be a part of it.

Timeline

ca. 3000 B.C.	The abacus is invented in China.
1642	Eighteen-year-old Blaise Pascal invents the Pascaline, a form of early adding machine.
1801	Joseph-Marie Jacquard invents the Jacquard loom, which uses punch cards.
1820–1840	Charles Babbage designs the first computing engines.
1890	The United States uses Herman Hollerith's invention in the national census and finishes the count in only six weeks.
1896	Herman Hollerith founds the Tabulating Machine Company.
1906	Lee De Forest invents the triode vacuum tube, which will power the first computers.
1941	Konrad Zuse invents the Z3, a programmable calculator, to help design airplanes and missiles.
1943	The British invent a top-secret computer, Colossus, to decode enemy messages.
1944	Howard H. Aiken, working with IBM, invents a computer-calculator, the Mark I.
1944–1945	John Presper Eckert and John W. Mauchly design ENIAC, the Electronic Numerical Integrator And Computer, a thousand times faster than the Mark I.
1945	The EDVAC, the Electronic Discrete Variable Automatic Computer, is designed. It is the first computer with memory.
1947	William Shockley, Walter Brattain, and John Bardeen invent the semiconductor.

continued next page

1951	Remington Rand markets the first commercial computer, the Universal Automatic Computer (UNIVAC).
1953	IBM is the first to design a mass-produced computer called the IBM 650.
1959	IBM is the first to design a solid-state—using transistors—computer, the 7090.
1960s	Several companies, including IBM and Sperry-Rand, as well as Honeywell and others, start designing computers to meet a growing demand.
1964	IBM's System/360 series of computers are the first to be compatible with each other.
1967	A chess-playing computer is made an honorary member of the United States Chess Federation.
1971	Intel designs the 4004 chip that makes the pocket calculator possible, allowing everyone to carry around the calculating power of a computer. Its success inspires Intel to work on better, smaller, and faster computer chips.
1975	The January issue of *Popular Electronics* announces the birth of the first true personal computer, the MITS Altair 8800 microcomputer. Bill Gates and Paul Allen start the company that will become Microsoft.
1977	Radio Shack releases the TRS-80, a popular personal computer. Apple Computer releases its first computer, the Apple II.
1980s	Hundreds of start-up companies begin designing so-called PC clones based on the IBM models. Most fail.
1981	Microsoft launches MS-DOS, its Disk Operating System. IBM launches its first PC, running on an Intel 8088 microprocessor and using MS-DOS. The Osborne 1, the first portable computer,

	is invented. Hayes Micromodem designs the first nonbusiness modem for the PC. Two million PCs are sold.
1982	Five and a half million PCs are sold. The Commodore 64 is introduced.
1983	*Time* Magazine names the personal computer its "Man of the Year."
1984	Apple Computers releases its Macintosh, or Mac. Dell Computers is founded.
1985	Gateway Computers is founded. Microsoft releases the first version of the Windows operating system.
1993	Intel launches its first Pentium chip.
Late 1990s	A major slowdown hits the computer and software industry.

Glossary

amplifier—a device for increasing a sound, or electric voltage or current

amplifying circuit—a device that strengthens an electrical current

baud—a unit of measurement used to indicate the number of bits per second that are transmitted

byte—a basic unit of computer memory

calculator—a device that performs mathematical computations

census—an official counting of a country's population

central processing unit—the processor or brains of the computer

Compact Disc—a nonmagnetic, polished metal disc with a

protective plastic coating, used to store music or computer data

computer chip—a small rectangle on which are embedded one or more computer transistors

dissipate—to disappear or to dissolve

electrode—a device that is a deliberate conductor of electricity

filament—a thin thread or wire

floppy disk—a round piece of flexible plastic film coated with ferric oxide (iron) particles that can hold a magnetic field

germanium—a brittle, crystal-like, gray-white metallic element

kilobyte—1,024 bytes

mainframe computer—a high-level computer, shared by several users who connect to the computer through computer terminals

microprocessor—an integrated circuit that contains the entire central processing unit of a computer on a single chip

software—the computer coded instructions that tell a computer what to do

solid-state technology—a system that consists chiefly or entirely of semi-conducting materials and components

tallying—counting up items to get a total

transistor—a part of an electric circuit that can serve as an amplifier or a switch

vacuum tube—a series of metal grids and electrodes in a glass or metal tube, from which all air has been removed and through which electrical current flows

To Find Out More

Books

Collier, Bruce and James MacLachlan. *Charles Babbage and the Engines of Perfection*. New York: Oxford University Press, 1998.

Northrup, Mary. *American Computer Pioneers*. Berkeley Heights, NJ: Enslow Publishers, 1998.

Parker, Steve. *Computers*. Austin, TX: Raintree/Steck Vaughn, 1997.

Sherman, Josepha. *Bill Gates: Computer King*. Brookfield, CT: Millbrook Press, 1999.

Wright, David. *Computers*. Tarrytown, NY: Benchmark Books, 1996.

Organizations and Online Sites

Cnet.com
http://www.cnet.com
This online site specializes in computers and technology. It provides product information and technology news.

Computer History Museum
Building T-12A
Moffett Federal Airfield
Mountain View, CA 94035
http://www.computerhistory.org
This museum is dedicated to the artifacts and stories of the information age.

The History of Apple Computers
http://www.apple-history.com/history.html
This online site provides an in-depth look at the history of Apple Computers.

Jones Telecommunications and Multimedia Encyclopedia
http://www.digitalcentury.com
This is a good site tracing the history of computing and PCs.

Triumph of the Nerds

http://www.pbs.org/nerds

This companion online site to a Public Broadcasting Service (PBS) documentary provides biographical information on the people behind the computer revolution.

ZDNet: Where Technology Takes You

http://www.zdnet.com

This site features articles about and reviews of new technology.

A Note on Sources

Both the Internet and several books were of great use in researching the history of the PC. Among the Internet sources that were especially useful was www.cnet.com, which is a site that specializes in information about computers and technology. Another really helpful site was www.pc-history.org, which is a good site tracing the history of the PC. And for those who haven't seen the PBS series on television, www.pbs.org/nerds is the web version of a documentary about the people behind the computer revolution.

As for useful books, I'd have to include my own book, *Bill Gates: Computer King*, since Microsoft played a major role in the development of the PC. *Direct From Dell: Strategies That Revolutionized an Industry*, by Michael Dell, founder of Dell Computers, is another useful book that is also fun to read. A good book on the people behind the computer revolution is Mary Northrup's *American Computer Pioneers*.

—*Josepha Sherman*

Index

Numbers in *italics* indicate illustrations.

About The Author

Josepha Sherman is an author, editor, and professional folklorist. For Franklin Watts, she has written two other Watts Library titles, *Internet Safety* and *The History of the Internet*. She has also written several biographies on important people in technology, including *Bill Gates: Computer King*, *Jeff Bezos*, and *Jerry Lang and David Philo: Chief Yahoos*. She has authored more than forty novels, including fantasy and science fiction.